BEFORE I EXPIRE

100 Days to inspire the Soul

LEE JOHNSON

This book is dedicated to my baby sisters Laura and Jamierra who were killed on the left side of me. Know that your death will inspire the world to stretch themselves while they still have time. As well as my mother, whom I love unconditionally. You continue to fight and battle. These words were for you before anyone else. Make no mistake this book was written by the four of us. Thank you for inspiring me to be greater than anything I've ever seen and to give more than I take from every moment this life offers.

Your soul knows who you really are, and the flesh is constantly deceiving you. Your job subsequently is to build a relationship with your soul, not your flesh. And like you, no one ever told me this and so I started most of my life believing it was about solely building a relationship with the physical me. That consumed most of my time and because I had neglected to find and build with my soul, I never met me. I never found myself because I only knew a marginalized and limited version of myself. I was completely dependent and directed by my emotions and what I "thought" was best. Hence, I was lost and unconscious. It took me a long time to identify that to be true in my life, and even longer to embrace. This book is designed to inspire you to build the inner you. Everyone focuses on the "outer" experience in life, but this *Before I Expire* journey helps us to remember that our life depends on us being completely engaged in our inner pursuit. In this internal pursuit, you will find the peace that passes understanding and capture constant moments that never allow you to waste another second of your life.

I remember when my mother told me the story of how I saved her life as she was about to commit suicide when I called her out of the blue and told her when she answered, "Mom I love you so much." She's battled substance abuse for most of her life. Its important to note for the sake of transparency that I never turned my back on my parents for their struggles nor mistakes. I was abandoned by my mother when I was 8 years old, and although most children develop anger toward their parents, I always understood that we all have our own equations to solve in this lifetime and in some gardens some seeds take longer to grow. My mom is still fighting at this very second, and as I constructed these days to save her life everyday, I speak to you as well. Nothing in your life will stop what God has designated for you. You need only to be in alignment with your soul and to constantly seek the face of God everyday before you expire.

As you begin to journey through these 100 days it is important to note that reading this will not give you the answers you desire, but it will lead you to the very doors that hold everything you've ever hoped for. The bible states that faith without works is dead, yet if one has the faith the size of a mustard seed, he or she can move mountains. This book serves as the faith. This is the fuel of hope that in addition must be coupled with the works to see its true value and effectiveness. Do not rush through these days for some and for others do not missed the value of the day because it seems simple. They overlooked Jesus and killed him because it was so simple that they missed what they had been waiting for. The only time you have is unknown, but I give you these days in hopes that you will discover spaces within yourself you never knew existed. God is taking you somewhere and if you're reading this, you're about to free yourself from a prison you didn't even know existed. Time starts now....

Day 1

"Destroy what Destroys You."

In an effort of pursuing true formlessness, I must remain open to the cyclical transitions' life presents. More than often it is the bondage of self that destroys the plasticity necessary for growth. Destroy what destroys you while becoming that which you seek before you expire.

Day 2

"The Distance between who you are and who you become is what you do."

So many people you know will tell you why it didn't work out or justify why they are in the dismal space life currently offers them. What most won't tell you is that they simply neglected to do what was necessary to produce the desired aim. Everyone talks good but if you measure the distance between who you are and who you become, it is approximated in what you do. Want to really change your life? Do more.

Day 3

"Fall in love with the journey. Make love to the details. Marry the process. Everyday."

The relationship we develop with ourselves requires the daily intentional investment of optimal truth, love and growth. Falling in love with the process caused me to fall into better versions of myself everyday. Don't attempt to hold on to anything on your journey holding you back. Unnecessary weight is just that.... unnecessary.

Day 4

"You cannot destroy what does not exist."

One cannot hit what his/or her eyes cannot see. We must first see the true obstacle to defeat the true obstacle. The greatest prisons ever built were the ones you and I built for ourselves. And most of us live most of our lives sadly never uncovering this internal truth. Your freedom must be as much of intentional as it is habitual. Will you decide to be free from yours?

Day 5

"Heal Your unhealthy habits"

Unhealthy habits begin to re-acclimate today in an effort to protect themselves from the new systems needed for this new space in your life. Embrace what is new by anchoring yourself in the accountability sector. If you mess up, continue to "practice" the goals you set until you create a tipping point, knowing that even in your hindsight assessment, that is indeed too a form of progress. *Be free and formless to everything.*

Day 6

"The goal is not to build this assuming image or projecting form. The goal is to be fluid and formless, like Water."

The worst thing you could do in your life is lock yourself in a room of stagnation without the key to get out and grow. Bruce Lee is famous for utilizing the analogy of water to lament the optics of true growth. It echoes the concept of being formless so that you might be able to take shape and new form to the better person you are always producing. Problem with many of us is we neglect to create the environment needed to grow. Particularly, internally. Be formless, each moment.

Day 7

"Where in the hell are you going, energy?"

Today, nor any day longer will I be deceived by myself and emotions. Where your focus goes your energy follows, yet sometimes our investments need re-alignment. And its healthy to embrace that truth because often, we are simply over-invested in the wrong things. The ability to objectively self-assess is priceless. *Don't forget to be free in managing the direction of your energy at all times.*

Day 8

"Create an appetite that forces you to throw up the old version of yourself daily."

Habits. Systems. Evolution. The revolution of the three will not be televised but could potentially cost you everything. Always make the decision to grow in any space, and curate better habits and systems that foster a more efficient you. You are only as good as the systems you abide in and we all have them. Whether, or not we improve those systems are completely contingent upon us.

Day 9

"Heightened perspectives birth expanded capacities. Be Free and anchored by the timelessness of your Soul."

Relationships that gave you the feeling of forever, exposed themselves for the temporary spaces they were worth. Yet, our ability to see the true value of a thing in all things is critical to optimal growth. Much of that value stems from timeless wisdom I received long ago, that every dot in your life is connected. Your job is not to understand how the dot got there, but why it is there for you. For example, it is not important that the relationship didn't work, but what's important was what were you able to learn and develop about yourself from that relationship. The real currency in life comes from all things both good, and bad because all dots are related.

Day 10

"You cannot think your way into new living, you must live your way into new thinking."

Even God tells us faith without works is dead. We try to utilize the faith and neglect the works necessary to activate it. This book is designed to fuel your faith, but to change your life will require the work. Yet combined, "I can do ALL things through Christ who strengthens me."

"If you're not who you are supposed to be for yourself, you can't be what you're supposed to be for others."

Day 11

"It *dawned on me, as God's raindrops divinely drip from my soul, that I should catch them and share them with the world. Its safe to say I made the right decision. Don't forget to be Free.*"

In this moment, I am reminded of the longitude and latitude of the soul. That I must continue to evolve without ceasing and seek beyond the grasp this world has imparted me to believe I am able to reach. While the anchor of my flesh beseeches me to remain in the confines of mediocre thinking and societal conformity, the compass I have dug from my soul shows me a direction of greater truth. Therefore, it is both the compass and the creator that has allowed me to truly become free. My purpose now is to help you navigate in hopes that you too will be *free and formless.*

Day 12

"At what point do we release ourselves and stop suffocating the Soul?"

People crave being famous, popular and important so much that they commit suicide to their souls everyday. Stop killing yourself establishing the wrong metrics in your life. I'm just saying, if you're breathing, you deserve to L I V E.

Day 13

"To climb outside a thought, one must first climb inside that thought."

Your mind forms patterns. The trick is identifying which patterns you operate in and improving those same patterns. Simple right? Behavioral pattern recognition. This will help you better synthesize your mind activity and manage your thoughts and decisions. Plus, if you don't know what game you're playing, you've lost before you've even begun. M I N D G A M E S.

Day 14

DREAM FURTHER

If you're going to dream, make sure you dream with your eyes open because you should always be looking for greater dreams to birth and build. And you'll know you're alive when you close your eyes and its brighter on the inside than it is on the outside *because your soul's truthful radiance is blinding.*

Day 15

"Always require first from yourself, what you require from others. Be Free."

We require the best from everyone else. We need our friends and relationships to be on point. We desire to drive the best cars, have the best phones, clothes and other material items. We have constructed the highest standards for everything and everyone except ourselves corroborated with accountability. Do you require yourself to give the best quality of *YOU* to the people and situations of your life? Don't forget to give more than you take from every relationship you encounter.

Day 16

"At some point in life you'll begin to connect all the dots in your life and realize that everything is connected to something. You'll embrace and grow from ALL of you and not just the appealing pieces."

Life becomes extremely dangerous when you stop discriminating between the good vs. bad in your life and just start embracing and growing from *ALL* things. This philosophy of living adopts supreme peace and fluidity within yourself and with others. *Be free.*

Day 17

"Some people can only exist in clutter. Moreover, even the subsections of our own lives we often create unbeknownst unhealthy habits that yield toxic results. Yet, many times these habits and processes are adopted from what has been modeled for us. Identify that which you emulate and evolve that shit before you expire!"

There are some people who only identify with the drama they create. Prone to permeating negativity underlined in narcissism and they can't see it. Really, its all they've seen during the maturation process, so they subconsciously replay the same emotional scenes. People that create hurt are 9 times out of 10 merely projecting their own internal message of hurt, *decoded*. Are you replaying any old scenes in your life, or relationships? Who hurt you?

Day 18

"Both Life and Looks can be deceiving."

It will never look like what you think it looks like. They knew the messiah was coming, but because Jesus didn't fit into their fragmented view of what the messiah looked and behaved as, *they missed him*. Like the messiah would never come as a carpenter, right!? But because he didn't fit into their microscopic absolute, they didn't just miss the messiah while he was among them, but they killed him. I'm telling you that what God has for you will never fit man nor woman's standards and if you're not careful, you wont just miss the blessing, but you'll kill it.

Day 19

"Don't forget. Embrace everything."

Sometimes the trajectory of your life won't be like everyone else's. In fact, it never will. Embrace your own speed, process and journey. This is not a race to see who gets "there" the quickest. We all die in the end.

Day 20

Which YOU are you?

As stated in the earlier chapters, if you don't know what game your playing you've lost before you've even begun. Please know that there are indeed two selves. You have the lower self which is your flesh that desires what it wants when it wants it. Sex, money, success and in an immediate manner. The higher self, which is your soul, doesn't care what kind of car you drive or if you have a four-year degree...Your soul only cares that you find it and stay connected to it. Always be increasingly engaged with which you, you're connected to. Use God as the compass.

"Failure of figuring out the language we speak usually results in us lying to ourselves."

Day 21

"There just absolutely isn't one life to live, **we've been bamboozled!**"

Historically, we've been funneled into this ant farm of thinking that there is only one life to live. Go to school. Get a job in your field. Pay taxes. But our modern juggernauts actually lament that one route alone projected onto 7 billion people in this world wont work. The billionaires of this world, *such Bill gates and Mark Zuckerberg,* dropped out of collegiate institutions to embark on their own society-shifting pathways. Jeff Bezos (the richest man in the world) who's mother had him at 17, left his job on Wallstreet and started a company out of his garage selling books online. Jay-Z was selling crack at 26 but would go on to be a leading financial, social and political figure of our time. Moral of the story? Discover other routes so that you can find there are multiple roads and highways, not just one!

Day 22

"I believe God can do anything because I've seen him do everything."

Our experiences, development and journey will all be solely contingent on the individual relationship we build with God. If you think that you've seen the best God has to offer in your life – no matter what age- then my friend, you don't know God. Every day his grace, mercy and blessings are new. And for someone else, if he did it before he can do it again.

Day 23

"Marriage vs. Dating"

The problem is you want to date God, and lack the element of commitment necessary to marry God; going all in. You like God, but you haven't fell in love because your flesh tells you to keep your options open. Stop dating your faith. Marry it!

Day 24

"It's not that deep!"

Every situation is not as deep as your mind makes it. Some fire we feel in situations are the result of us increasing our own temperature. Let's explore operating with *more empathy* and *less self*. Check yourself the same way you're so quick to voice your dismay to someone else. Fostering more accountability in this space spews development on the highest level. Plus, most of the time you'll it's just not that deep.

Day 25

"There aren't any receipts on Life."

Today you will get the absolute *MOST* out of your life and repeat this for the rest of your life. Why? Because once you stop breathing, there aren't any receipts to exchange and take your life back!

Day 26

"Undefeated Help"

Help me to forgive, love, and constantly grow God. Help me to seek more of you even in the times that I don't feel like looking. Help me to realize you've been undefeated since before you created the heavens and the earth. God, all I need is the help you give unconditionally.

Day 27

"Relativity"

Time is relative. Your journey, goals and dreams will experience a peculiar duration and that's ok, given your chapters have been tailor made for your story. I love using the traffic light for lessons in this case embracing the uniqueness of our own selves. The yellow light doesn't try to be the red light, and the green light isn't interested in the red lights journey. Why? Because they were each made with a different purpose. You never have to compare your journey to another's. You have your own light.

Day 28

"At some point the goal must become the seed."

We set out for the goal, but at some point, the goal must evolve into the seed because the blessing will birth a blessing. Never settle and know there is more growth to experience as a seed who's waiting to blossom. No limits. No capacity. Only an infinite God who has made you in his infinite image.

Day 29

"Sum of Life"

Sometimes the best addition you can make to your life's equation is a subtraction. And you don't even need to know math to solve this problem. Now ask yourself, "What am I willing to take away?"

Day 30

"Manipulating My Pain"

Stop hiding your pain, it only hurts your healing. Rather than let that be the reason you stop, let it fuel the reason for why you keep going. This component in life really is a distraction to take your attention away from how powerful you really are. Think of the time you felt your lowest compared to the time you felt on top of the world. The person never changed, only the temperature. Manipulate your pain to work to your advantage in life. Be strategic with how you manage and grow yourself.

"Most people never find themselves because to discover oneself means you really have to see yourself."

Day 31

"The Power of Patience."

With God, sometimes your power isn't in your power, but in your patience. The power isn't in your ability, but your availability to God's timing and purpose for your life. Oh, and in case you don't see it, this is going to be an amazing year for you! Go get it!

Day 32

"Two cars cannot Fit into One Parking Space"

Note to self: Today, with God's help, no matter what I face, I will let faith and trust be my first response, *not fear!* Because I know that two cars can not fit in one parking space. I must always be intentional in driving and parking my thoughts.

Day 33

"Truth"

Sometimes the most powerful truth is simply being able to identify what's draining you. And when you find it, be strong enough to let it go. Now, this becomes an interesting dichotomy when you discover YOU to be the one draining you. At that point you have to make a decision to kill that piece of yourself that is detrimental to all that you were meant to become. Breathe....now let that shit go!

Day 34

"Holiday Gifts"

The gift you should give yourself each day is the gift of giving more to others than you take. You may not be reaping any fruit in your life because you simply haven't sown the seeds. If you should attempt to out give God for the rest of your life…. that's when everything changes.

Day 35

"Don't Drown"

You can either be your own wave today or drown trying to ride someone else's. Some of us are merely swimming in waters we simply don't belong. The choice is yours, but whatever you do, don't drown.

Day 36

"Spaces and Repeats"

The space between every failure and success is beautifully woven with wisdom, and destiny. We just repeat what we don't understand, until we understand why we were repeating it in the first place.

Day 37

"No more Suicide."

You want to be rich and famous so bad that you commit suicide to your soul every day. This need to be seen and validated by society has become cancerous. Yet, the only thing worse than someone else killing you is you killing yourself. Live in everyday and everything you do by challenging what you crave to satisfy your life's pallet. The goal is not to be successful…the goal is to become. Stay alive by always outgrowing old thoughts and habits. Unhealthy thoughts kill more people than car accidents.

Day 38

"Broke"

There are so many broken individuals that don't know they're broken, and consequently go around breaking other people. We need more healing, love and restoration. But first, we must acknowledge and identify that we are internally broken.

Day 39

"First Impressions"

Life is so funny. You think you know yourself until you meet yourself for the first time 20, 30, 40 years after you've been breathing.

Day 40

"Parking Faith"

It would kill most of us to admit the harsh truth of how much of our own time we don't value and waste. Until we get that call or go to that funeral. We're all so sad and will be at more family functions until two weeks pass then we revert to business as usual. Stop wasting your time. Value those relationships. Love yourself. And remember you're on the clock!

"If you know the enemy and know yourself, you need not fear the result of a hundred battles. If you know yourself but not the enemy, for every victory gained you will also suffer a defeat. If you know neither the enemy nor yourself, you will succumb in every battle."

~ Sun Tzu, The Art of War

Day 41

"Swim Higher"

It seems like the world is drowning in "average" and quite frankly, that's a sad way to die. I also found that to know yourself is one thing, but to continue to find secret spaces God hid within you is a completely higher way of life. Swim Higher.

Day 42

"Prison"

The only chains that exist in our lives are the ones we ourselves create. Many believe the goal in life is to be rich or successful, but truthfully the goal is to be free from the prisons we create for ourselves. Be Free.

Day 43

"Broken Concrete"

God please break the concrete of myself that keeps blocking me from you. Very often the justifications we use are illusive excuses which keep most from being what is most important.... Accountable! Much of what one says and what one does will often differ. And they will try to excuse it or justify it by saying its concrete when its really a paper plate. What's the point? Don't hide yourself inside of concrete and say I'm supposed to be this way. Rather, always break the concrete of who you are to ensure it is concrete inside and not a paper plate!

Day 44

"Language Barriers"

God help me to see that my flesh and soul speak two different languages. If I interpret the voice of my journey, I must always be aware of what I'm communicating to the soul of who I am, if at all. The language of my core will guide me in even seeing pieces of myself that are counterproductive or ill. This personal relationship that I grow and develop with myself can exist only with clear communication. What inspires you? What are you afraid of? You must know these things so that you may be proactive and not reactive when they become relevant on your path. A proactive system is better than a reactive solution. Knowing the language, you speak prevents things within before they even transpire. What language do you speak?

Day 45

"Tragic"

When you die, the tragedy will not exist in what you didn't accomplish. The tragedy will only exist in the fact that you didn't believe that you could accomplish anything with God, faith and hard work. Miss the tragedy today and everyday for the rest of your life! B E L I E V E.

Day 46

"Power"

After all that you've been through, stop forgetting that nothing in life could ever break you. You're stronger than you think you are. Today you'll access your power by remembering how much God gave you in the first place.

Day 47

"Inevitable Control"

I've got to believe it's going to work out because God can't and won't fail me. It's just not possible. So even when it's not going my way, I must always know that it's always going God's way. There is never a moment God is not in control.

Day 48

"V I E W S"

You must begin to see yourself outside of yourself to remain open to all the possibilities of who God intended you to become. Implement forms of meditation in your life that will help you detach from yourself because the view in the crowd is far different from the view of the crowd from 10,000 feet in the air. These are the practices most wont do. Disconnect from yourself to find the views of you.

Day 49

"Crossroads"

Injecting love and forgiveness onto the intersection of pain and tribulation yields fluid growth. Having a tough time forgiving those that hurt you? Remember you break God's heart everyday too, but he loves you unconditionally. *Forgive and Love* M O R E.

Day 50

"Lifetime Student"

I must seek and identify each lesson in life intentionally as if I was searching for a breath to live. Learning yields the highest production of growth and that is the element I should constantly exercise more than anything. I must always remain a student of the journey.

"A lot of people and circumstances tried to bury you in life…. What they didn't know was that you were a seed."

Day 51

"Who are you looking for?"

Never stop searching for more of yourself. More of you really means less of you, and more of God. Be intentional everyday in what you're seeking in this life.

Day 52

"God's Irony"

It's funny how the failures, fears and doubts that were once walls become doors that introduce you to that which you've been seeking this entire journey. God's infinite wisdom at it's finest.

Day 53

"Character Construction"

I never knew how much building inner character would help destroy inner doubt. Nevertheless, sowing into the character will grow you closer to the soul. It is the very substance of your life that enables you to be anchor in what really matters in this lifetime. I believe much of our character is predicated on our values and love for self. If you love something quite naturally you want to see it grow and flourish. This also means that if you really want to see whatever that thing is grow, then you must also be willing to do what is necessary for the growth. You'll find the construction of self, to be a daily investment, but it is more than worth it.

Day 54

"No More Locked Doors"

We are all looking to unlock the next door in our life, but those doors will always require you to first unlock a piece of yourself before you unlock it. So, before you expire embrace every possibility of exposing yourself to something new. There are so many more experiences and people for you to meet. Exposure also gives us the actual space to grow and expand with every lesson learned. No more locked doors!

Day 55

"Strategic Water"

Who knew the tears you cried would seep into the cracks of who you are and reach the seed God planted? Have faith that the water you need may not come from a water faucet or bottle.

Day 56

"Language Living"

The "English" of one's words often differs from the "Spanish" of one's actions. The alignment of these two languages will free you. Yet, what most say will indeed vary from what one does. Be free, and trust God for the next level of your life.

Day 57

"What Distraction?"

"Distractions don't look like distractions, until they're done distracting you." I wonder how much of the only time I have is being wasted with distractions I've deemed necessary to breathe. Today Identify every disguised distraction in your life. Set it all on fire.

Day 58

"Stillness"

Sometimes the next step in life is simply being still and trusting God. Gods ways are not our ways nor, time our time. Plus, real faith is keeping the vehicle of our mind parked in God's driveway of destiny and purpose for our lives, *even when we want to drive off.* Peace be still.

Day 59

"Fly Fire Drills"

Your quality of life and the value thereof will almost always be directly correlated to the choices you make. And the choices you don't make are just as valuable as the ones you do. Take being prepared for example, a choice. I remember being in elementary school and we had what may remember as a *fire drill.* The principal would let us know that we would be having a practice drill randomly at some point. In this simulation we would practice exactly what we would do in case of a real fire so that when one did occur, we would be prepared in being proactive and not reactive. Practice for the real before real occurs. And I found my life being like that same fire drill or the lack of. Time and time again I was reacting to the events in my life, not understanding that raw reaction was only scratching the itch of my flesh. I had to implement fire drills in my life. As a result, you will be prepared for any fire.

Day 60

"The Arrow"

"You cannot hit two targets with one arrow. If your thoughts stray, you miss the enemy's heart. The mind and arrow must become one. Only with such concentration of mental and physical power can your arrow hit the target and pierce the heart."

Day 61

"Element Opinions"

Some people just won't get it. Stop expecting the water to start a fire. Rather, embrace the truth of you being able to light your own flame.

Day 62

"Just Breathe"

You don't need the air they're trying to take from you to breathe. It would choke you to death in the first place. Give yourself permission to be free through the source from which all things flow. *Breathe.*

Day 63

"Accountability Anchor"

Never forget how many times you let YOU down. It keeps one grounded and operating in gratitude for God's constant grace and mercy. An anchor of accountability could stop the weight of the world.

Day 64

"Stay Involved in your Journey."

What's the use of the journey if you're not even looking? You will miss everything God is showing you because you didn't know that a sizable piece of your journey is a tour. Yea. God is taking you on a tour of yourself your entire life and showing you as he is growing you. Stay involved in your journey by always paying attention to the signs and symbols God offers you.

Day 65

"TRUTH x FACTS"

An undervalued asset is being able to acknowledge, "My truth that I'm living or believing is a lie." Then being able to be ok with being wrong, while being inspired and motivated to only operate in truth. It's ok to be wrong if you are genuinely seeking truth.

Day 66

"It's Okay"

It's okay to finally forgive that person you thought you forgave but never really did. Especially, if that person is you.

Day 67

"Language"

Sometimes the language to the solution has nothing to do with what comes out of our mouths, but everything to do with our ability to speak to the gaps within ourselves daily. What language are you speaking in your life?

Day 68

"Lose Yourself"

It's okay to lose the toxic unhealthy pieces of ourselves. It's ok to lose parts of yourself for the right reasons and garner optimal growth. A formidable solution? Lose yourself, then find yourself.

Day 69

"Push and Pull"

Today I will PULL the value out of everything that PUSHES me away. I will no longer combat conflict. I choose to truly embrace everything, whether it pushes or pulls me. This induces optimal growth and development. Because you chose to learn from everything life chose to give you.

Day 70

"HELP"

God help me to see it's really me in my own way. Help me guide and navigate when my flesh tells me "I can do this on my own." Help me to stop suffocating the breaths of my soul. All I ever needed was your help and yet still you gave your son. *Divine Help.*

Day 71

"God's Plan"

The years of your problems will be solved in the seconds of God's solutions. Remember, it only takes a move from God to move everything in your life for YOU!

Day 72

"Walls don't build walls...Bricks Do"

Most people undervalue perspective not realizing how we view a thing largely dictates how we deal with it. And so most people try to build a wall in life when all you must do is lay a brick. And brick by brick eventually you'll get a wall. This is the process of life. Lay a brick a day and you can build whatever wall you want in your life. And commit. Not just a year but 5 or 10 years.

Day 73

"Trust your Road"

Trust your journey. Though there are certain equations you've yet to solve, you can abide in the truth that God has divinely planted seeds on your path that will bloom in due season, if you faint not. He knew you before he formed you (Jeremiah 1:5) and has already taken care of everything. So, relax, *it's going to be ok.*

Day 74

"Jump"

Today, go to the edge of you are and jump into the possibilities of everything you are becoming. There will be times when standing on what you believe in will not be enough and you will have to jump!

Day 75

"Homeless"

You can either evict fear and doubt from the house of your mind, or it will burn it down. Contrary to popular belief, some things in your life are meant to be thrown out on the street. It may not seem like it, but I promise you don't need the rent "worrying" is paying you.

Day 76

"Divine Gardens"

Don't ever lose faith in the garden God is growing with you. Some seeds take longer to grow. And let's not forget the order of operations. You reap what you sow, but if you haven't sown in the pre-season then you can't reap in due-season. What seeds are you planting in your preseason? Now try sowing and telling God he doesn't have to give you a thing back and mean it…. Blessings start thickening at that point.

Day 77

"Controlling Thoughts"

Think about this. God's love through his son Jesus Christ, was engineered to carry the weight of any sin you could ever commit. He knew you before you knew you. Trust your journey knowing that God is in control and has been carrying you the entire time.

Day 78

"Eternal Water"

As so a single rain drop is to the ocean, so shall your time here on earth drip onto eternity. While you're here, make it count and give more than you take. For it is so that we are merely passing through.

Day 79

"We'd Rather Fill Spaces than Heal Spaces"

It's ok to let go of the old versions of yourself. God's holding you anyway. It's just that we'd rather fill spaces than heal spaces.

Day 80

"Rates"

The rate at which you grow will be largely be contingent upon your rate and capacity to love. Unconditional love to self and others will not only grow you, it will free you.

Day 81

"Things"

Sometimes the "thing" that you thought was for you was only the "thing" to prepare you for the "thing".

Day 82

"Keep"

There are always two sections to your seeking. Look within yourself and then disconnect from yourself to see you outside of yourself. This is objectivity at its best. Moreover, balanced perspectives foster optimal growth. Keep seeking, keep growing, and when you feel like you can't, still "Keep".

Day 83

"Blockage"

More than often "I" am the obstacle blocking me from me. The fluidity and concept of being free transcends this humanistic gap; And so as much as I die to myself daily, I must also grow from myself daily.

Day 84

"Open"

You're going to be as successful as you are willing to open your mind. A closed and restricted perspective creates a capacity for marginalized thinking. Challenge yourself everyday by exploring new ways to examine who you are and how you will impact the lives of the people you share space with here on earth. As you grow you will see your inspire others to be free and open.

Day 85

"God's Uber"

It will never look like what we think it should. You were waiting for God to pull up in an 18-wheeler, but you missed it because God sent an Uber. No worries, God is sending your uber back around!

Day 86

"Childish"

Many of us are hurting and that very hurt stems from the trauma of our childhood. Take God back to the place "it" happened and start the healing you deserve. What did you learn? How did it grow you? These questions will help you unpackage whatever that thing is draining the emotional and physical life out of you. Its ok to allow yourself to be honest enough with yourself to say what hurt you and how it made you feel. I had to go back and allow myself the proper healthy space to grieve. Although I was never upset with my parents, any 8-year-old that gets left or starving would be sad right? Because I thought I never felt it, I also thought the truth wasn't worth examining. Biggest mistake of my life. Inspect the pieces of your own story everyday and you will constantly discover blind spots interwoven in your journey. After all, not healing anymore is childish.

Day 87

"Metrics"

Stop measuring dead things.

Day 88

"Whose Time is this?"

Honestly, the way I've squandered and gave away money you would have guessed I never worked for it. The way I dismissed the hurt in my life and hence opportunity to heal you would have thought I never endured it. The amount of time I wasted while I was still breathing you would've sworn it wasn't never mine spewing questions such as…. "Whose time is this again?"

Day 89

"Style matters in how you live on your journey"

There is a stylistic component that separates you from everyone else around you. When you start to embrace the trinkets of your journey, things become clear and the process is more fulfilling. So, have you identified what makes you? And not the common responses that everyone gives that only shows still that we are the same. Want to change your life? Constantly ask yourself what make you, you and then evolve that every day of your life.

Day 90

"Formless Nature"

I'm searching for a space in time that acknowledges greatness to be a social norm and not the consequence of a particular group. And so with the time I have left, I'm trying to help people find and build relationships with their soul. I found out how weak and deceptive my OWN flesh was, which made me become formless. My life is now a symbol for others to be free, even in the bondage life often imposes upon us. *Be formless.*

Day 91

"Be allergic to Air"

And yet my flesh wants to breathe air more than it wants to drown in God. I believe it's the inevitable battle we all must face. The world tells me I must breathe to live, and yet God tells me to die daily to the flawed forms of myself. And so today, let the choices of your soul and the direction of your heart be anchored in the ocean of the Holy spirit.

Day 92

"Never forget how we always forget."

You finally got the job you needed to pay your bills and get your head above water. You were passionate and appreciative that God Blessed you. 30 days later you're always irritated and complaining about the company. What really happened whether it be 30 days or 10 years? More than often we forget why we needed that thing in the first place. We forget why we fell in love with that person to begin with. In every space of your life.... Never forget how we always forget.

Day 93

"The Power is in your Positioning."

Breathe. Now take a second to think about all of things we ask from God. We ask for the blessing, or the "place" but rarely do we ask for positioning for the place. God will never put you in a place he hasn't positioned you for. Don't look to get the place before you've found your positioning.

Day 94

"Don't love the branch more than the Tree."

You can exude confidence and still not know who you are. Confidence is a branch, not the tree. You do not need to be confident in whether your heart beats, one only needs to acknowledge and be. When those components become anchors, an ocean of confidence will birth itself.

Day 95

Lifecycle

Life is cyclical, meaning that it is full of roundabouts, transitions and redundancy. Just learn to identify the various constant highs and lows. Learn to find the balance in all things. Suddenly, transitions become euphoric, full of daily enlightenment. You don't need all the answers to move forward.

Day 96

"How's Your Driving"

Getting mad at life and worrying about bills and drama is like getting mad that the light turned red. It's just part of the light and it serves a purpose. Don't get mad at the red light. Focus and rewire the way you respond to things. Because all things are merely blocks that build you. Keep Building. Keep Driving.

Day 97

"Stupid Stuff?"

It's extremely difficult to live a long life and not do something stupid. And we all must live with the consequences of our stupid decisions, often trapped repeating the same mistakes falling victim to a toxic system of thinking. But what's ironic about life is that wisdom uses those exact "stupid" moments to learn, grow and evolve you. Life is about making mistakes, stupid calls, and bad judgements and then using those very things to transform your life. Or maybe you're not feeling me and think all of this is nothing more than a bunch of stupid stuff.

Day 99

"Learn to Look at things Different"

Are you able to see yourself outside of who you think you are? The truth is that there are simply some spaces of yourself that you can't see without someone's help and some truth that differs from who you thought you were. It's okay. The more refined and developed version of you is supposed to look different from how you initially saw you.

Day 98

"Tough Love"

It may seem unfathomable for parents to abandon their kids or allow them to go hungry for weeks. Maybe your father told you he wished you were never born or spat on you. While your mother left you in the cold as a child eating cream of corn out of the can? I'm sure that you've endured more than this, but I need you to know that you can't expect something from God that you aren't willing to give yourself. He forgives you everyday as you break God's heart the same way your parents broke yours. The essence of unconditional love is that it bears no limits. I love my mom more than anything because the strongest form of love is displaying the same love God displays to us each day; that is loving someone whose actions may not deserve it. It's called tough love.

"The Last Day"

I remember it every day as if it were yesterday. We were only supposed to be going to the corner store and coming back home. However, no one in that car could have anticipated what was about to take place and that it would change the complete trajectory of our lives. My Dad was driving, and my mother was in the passenger seat. I sat in the back in the middle with my two sisters on my left Laura, and Jamierra. My brother Gregory was on my right. Then it happened. We were hit by an 18-wheeler and my two sisters were killed instantly. Just like that it was all over for them and I would come to find that one of my greatest tragedies would be the very vehicle God would use to help me help others be free. It would inspire me to come to a pivotal realization that it was disrespectful to the opportunity of life not value my time or get the most out of myself every single day when my sisters didn't get that opportunity. I found that it was disgraceful not to be the best expression of myself to inspire my mother as she was still solving her life toughest equation. In all of this, God would use my story to change the lives of people all over the world before they expired simply by reflecting the only luxury of life……. time. We just don't know how much time we have here. Before you expire it is my hope that this read pushes you to continue to grow and evolve everyday. So that when your time comes, you can have peace knowing that you were fully engaged and present as God took you on the greatest ride of your life.

48132802R00067

Made in the USA
Columbia, SC
06 January 2019